Bamboo Church

The Hugh MacLennan Poetry Series

Editors: Kerry McSweeney and Joan Harcourt
Selection Committee: Donald H. Akenson, Philip Cercone,
Allan Hepburn, and Carolyn Smart

TITLES IN THE SERIES

BAMBOO CHURCH

Ricardo Sternberg

McGill-Queen's University Press
Montreal & Kingston · London · Ithaca

ISBN 0-7735-2566-1

Legal deposit second quarter 2003
Bibliothèque nationale du Québec

Printed in Canada on acid-free paper that is 100% ancient forest
free (100% post-consumer recycled), processed chlorine free.

McGill-Queen's University Press acknowledges the
support of the Canada Council for the Arts for our
publishing program. We also acknowledge the financial
support of the Government of Canada through the Book
Publishing Industry Development Program (BPIDP) for
our publishing activities.

**National Library of Canada Cataloguing
in Publication**

Sternberg, Ricardo, 1948–
Bamboo church / Ricardo Sternberg.
Poems.
ISBN 0-7735-2566-1
I. Title.
PS8587.T4711B35 2003   C811'.54   C2003-900614-X
PR9199.3.S78485B35 2003

This book was typeset by Dynagram Inc.
in 10/13 New Baskerville.

for Chrissy

Queres ler o que
tão só se entrelê
E o resto em ti está?

Jorge de Lima

CONTENTS

BAMBOO CHURCH

TWO WINGS

She would drift into the kitchen
trailing fragments of a hymn that spoke of God,
a river, the pair of golden wings
that would be hers on Judgement Day
and were you to look at her then
you might well decide your best bet
for a meal would be to eat out:

she was blind and appeared a little lost
in her tile and linoleum kingdom.
But she vaguely addressed the garlic,
the onion, the tomato and between her hands
rubbed a spring of rosemary over olive oil.
A fragrance then arose and you decided
you had best sit down. And you did.

Did you fall asleep? Did you dream?
You awoke to the smart snap of sails:
the billowing of a tablecloth.
She returned and a generous bowl
was placed in front of you.
Then she crossed her arms and waited:
her prayer done, your eating was its Amen.

PAULITO'S BIRDS

In dozens of plain cages
each with its mirror and bell
my great uncle raised birds
but the steepled bamboo church
with a nest in its hollow pulpit
he, the fierce atheist,
kept for the mating pair.

At his whim, admonished
not to speak, I followed,
acolyte with burlap bag
from which he doled out
ceremonious, almost sacramental,
feed to the fluttering tribe.

Half his thumb was gone:
a loss he would ascribe
– in a sequence meant to mirror
my own small failings –
first, to sucking his thumb,
next, to teasing the parrot
and later to being careless
around the carpentry tools.

Perhaps it was his demeanour
– dry stick of a man – or the way
the door to the birds was locked
and he alone kept the key;

perhaps it was that stump of a thumb
grudgingly displayed when we sat
at the table and the stubborn
afternoon refused to move,

that brings him back today
as wizard, magus, *bruxo*,
who, against ransom not received,
holds locked in this spell
of feathers and birdseed,
the children of his kingdom.

PARABLE

Disguised as a camel
the millionaire broke
through the gates
of heaven.

Brazen, that camel
brayed in the choir,
sang his rough hosannas
out of key.

Good grief
cried God
and then stared
in disbelief.

But only when
down on earth
at the circus
a clumsy camel

failed to thread
the needle's eye,
was the gatecrasher
recognized,

stripped of harp,
halo and wings
then sent hurtling
into darkness.

QUARK

Consider the quark: its existence
is posited by scientists entranced
by a nothing which is there;
a particle that does not share
the known properties of materiality:
there but not there: a ghost entity.

Cyril of Thessalonika argued this case:
God withdrew and thus freed space
for the expanding universe. Absence
was his gift which makes his presence
this oxymoron worthy of contemplation:
the Zero at the core of all creation.

FIRST DANCE

Such a wealth of buttocks
would have slowed the walk
of anyone but (praise be to God!)
it proved mere ballast

to the strut of Aunt Dolores.
When music revved her hips
she moved and still would move
long after the exhausted boys

had surrendered the floor, and more,
even with the band gone silent.
Her snapping fingers then the beat,
melody, her deep-throated hum.

Inveterate dancer,
what dance didn't you know?
The Boogie-Woogie, Calypso,
Castle Walk, the Lindy Hop,

Fox-trot, Samba and Tango,
the Polka, Waltz and, drunk,
a mean Hully-Gully, a raw
down and dirty Rock & Roll.

Half her size, my uncle
was the only man I saw
do justice to her style.
Once – and only once –

on any given night
he would drop his cards
to sidle towards her on the floor.
A tiny god, enthroned

in the haze of his Gauloise,
he held her mesmerized.
His moves pared now
into a sizzling stance:

a suggestive sway of the hips,
a licentious thrust of the belly,
the head thrown back, towards heaven,
a rooster, set to let loose

the fierce light of a brand new day.
He stood defiant, belligerent,
though their blissful marriage
was twenty years old.

At some wedding or another
(I must have been eight)
she called me to the floor
and at my hesitation

sashayed, picked me up
and held me close. When since
have I so been whirled
or returned to that space

a body learns to inhabit
in the lull between two beats?
Locked within her arms
I was danced.

He cries from the left eye, forever
bemoaning tides, the luminous
rings round the dark of the moon.
Frozen, his world is a dead mobile.

Stranded in a northern latitude,
he brays for deliverance, begs
for a balm to assuage the heart.
A slow stomp round a crude altar

and he offers up slivers of fingernails,
the rough incence of matted hair.
He shakes his beard and the bones
of small birds drop to the floor.

But these oblations get no answer
and allegiance shifts to another god.
What new rituals must he now invent
as he turns his howl into a dainty canticle?

Far from all that's green and of easy flourish
the beast becomes a long lament
as he awaits the advent of weather
that can set that mobile in motion again.

NOAH'S WIFE

Sometime, somewhere,
the seed of tears
dropped into her eyes.

At first it amused us:
this collecting of tears
in matchboxes, shoe-

boxes, in suitcases.
I set tears in rings,
She strung necklaces.

An abacus of tears
marked the days we shed
and the years flowed by.

In the blue air of tears
we both grew older and tired;
mildew rewrote my books,

the canary moulted;
with one last miaow,
the cat moved out.

Only her ferns did well.
Enough, I decided.
Dry-eyed and resolute

she helped me pack
a humid suitcase
and we walked outside.

There, in a sudden gesture,
– as if scattering imaginary feed
to imaginary chickens –

she produced the sign
of a cloudless covenant:
this rainbow thrown above my hat.

MULE

Watch it gain substance
as the sun
burns brain fog away.

Here is the brown field,
here, under the shade
of the olive tree, the mule.

More than gravity, *gravitas*
holds this mule earthbound.
Ages ago it said goodbye

to illusions. Today it dreams
of stones, sunshine, hay.
A no-nonsense clopper

with slow, socratic eyes
too wise for foolishness,
too gentle for spurs,

it insists this easy gait
and a stubborn patience
will take us far.

We have barely begun
and, reader, already
you fidget in the saddle.

But who is to blame?
You were forewarned
and have no right

to ask this mule
to be what it is not.
This is no poem for you.

Close the book, then,
roll over and go to sleep.
Fashion out of dreams

why not a bicycle
then peddle quickly
all the way to hell.

PLATEIA KYRIAKOU

Blessings upon the crone
who every afternoon
feeds the cats of Molivos
for they are many
and they are all hungry.

Bowlegged and in black,
whiskers on her own face,
with a slow, laboured gait
she crosses the square
and where she sits, they congregate.

A spoonful for each cat.
(Is this food or sacrament?)
And once she's done she bangs
the empty tins like cymbals
and the cats are gone.

Levering herself against a knee
she struggles to stand up
then soothing a rheumatic hip,
she keeps to the leafy shade,
when it's her turn to leave the square:

a curse thrown to the gods
for having left to fate
(such poor provider)
the many cats of Molivos,
and they are all hungry.

CROWS

What I heard is this:
if perchance a crow
perched on the chimney
of the old Olive Press
– today the OP Hotel and Bar –
be touched by the first
fiery ray of sunlight,
arrayed in bright feathers
he would, with new voice,
sing out such a melody
village girls would weep
then consecrate themselves
to a religion that held him
to be god. And so it is

that a beat before daybreak
in raucous overflight
of sleeping Molivos
(asleep and intertwined
we are crow and sunlight)
they streak from the hills
so as to be the very first
on that chimney's rim.

Small comfort you say
for the obsolete eyesore
that mars our view
of Molivos, Lesbos, Greece.

JONAH

He, who would not show
his face to Moses,
who drove poor Job
to the brink of despair
comes to pester me now
disguised in the shape
of this minute insect.

No doubt he is making
inordinate demands:
that I build him an ark
or slay my first born
or move to the suburbs
where, covered in ash,
I impress upon the deaf
the magnificence of the word.

Who can decipher this buzz,
save that it signals his anger.
I know enough to stay awake:
dreams return me to the boat
that rocks, unsteady,
until that sailor is cast
into the maw of a giant fish.

Tomorrow, forthwith, to Nineveh.

MOUSE

What is the mouse to me
that I should now regret
his death

who, with such delight,
cocked the trap
that did him in?

Thief of the unswept crumb,
of cereal dust
that sifts to the floor;

burglar-*mignon*
I feel I need
do something to atone:

place your broken body
atop a flaming pyre
while my daughter blows

something blue
on her golden saxophone;
or, a lettuce leaf your shroud,

the trap is now the raft
I set adrift
on Lake Ontario.

But then suffer second thoughts:
oh this foolish mouse
and three times oh this foolish man

a wave of victory
cresting in his chest
as, with the tea-leaves and eggshells

of the kitchen trash,
trap and all,
I dispose of him.

GARDEN PRIMER

Carrots, said my grandfather,
are nails
which keep the field
from flying.

Then sunflowers,
said my grandmother,
are daughters
to the sun:

they stare and follow
their bright star father
then shed these hard
dark tears.

DANCER

In the darkness of my closet
she broods and whispers
let me out, let me out
I will war against the dust.

She is my last Victorian
– now my great-aunt is dead –
prim and proper though
her skirt is made of straw.

Unbending spinster,
you cannot hide from me
the sheer delight
sweeping brings to you.

Show me the two small feet
you keep forever hidden
so one can never tell
when they begin to dance.

Once upon a time
sun, wind and rain
could not keep their hands
from straying through your hair.

Now your fate is to wait
and to do so in the dark
until at last you hear the call
that breaks the spell:

Oh sweet maiden
cloistered in my closet,
it is finally Saturday.
Come dance with me.

I

Grief came to a woman
in her dream of a nightingale:

the blurred image of her mate
resolved itself into a thing of fangs.

How sing under such weather?
arte povera, arte povera.

Rhetoric torqued to a whisper,
the lunar syntax of dispossession

stuck in the throat of the meek.
She strikes a rhythm off turtle shells;

she rattles seeds in a dry gourd.
She holds the heart to this thin diet

until it composes itself again:
sleek idler in the Florida Keys.

II

Solar is now the enterprise
that holds her to this dance:

a woman may rock back and forth,
back and forth, steady as the beat

of the ocean's heart but not know
what brought, what kept her here:

aimlessness is an art and has a way
of getting you, always, somewhere

but at the shore a woman quickly need
reinvent footsteps the tide erased.

Still, wired to the seasons
for this brief, singular moment

she sings for the sake of singing
this storm this engine this love.

SUPPLY = DEMAND

Quarter to four on a Sunday
as the snow began to fall,
she entered the room and whispered
I wish for once and for all,

you'd tell me how much you love me
and how long that love will last
for doubt has crept into my heart
and passion is fading fast.

My love is a little machine
that's always set to GO;
it runs off a battery of kisses
but the battery is getting low.

My love is a little machine
but it's running cold today.
Join me in bed and let me
stroke all your doubts away.

Oh not so fast my darling.
I'm not easily assuaged;
when I saw your wandering eye
it drove me to such rage

that I chewed seven boxes of pencils
and painted my toe-nails black
then mixed a toxic cocktail
and prepared to bivouac

outside the gates of Melancholy
in the country of Despair
in the house whose name is Grief
and end my suffering there.

If my wandering eye offends
then I'll pluck it out in haste
But I swear to you my darling
your suspicions are misplaced.

A steadier heart has no man
who ever loved or wrote
and if I seem distracted
and at times appear remote

it's the law of love and business,
it's as Adam Smith commands:
I've restricted the supply
in the face of low demand.

MARCEL

Allow this irony to stand:
that a poem should praise you
who have no use for words,
you whom a spotlight holds
on the darkened stage.

Black pants, striped shirt,
white gloves, whiteface:
stripped of individuality
but not of character:
Marcel as Everyman.

Opening the door
– warped and contrary,
it resists your push
then suddenly yields
sending you reeling inside –
you enter your house.

Taking hold of the idea of broom,
you sweep away the idea of dust
and offer us this conundrum:
the objects you invoke
appear on stage yet never leave
the realm of pure ideas.

Free from the coarseness of form
they remain immutable and perfect.
Not the table but its essence
upon which you now carefully lay,
first that billowing tablecloth,
then, fragrant and steaming,
the idea of broth and of spoons
in the house of the hungry.

THE ANT

... ants have been growing fungus in gardens
and eating it for millions of years.

As a washerwoman
back from the river
balances on her head
the loaf of laundry,

so too does the ant
return to the hill
encumbered
by a large crumb.

Such a hunger
could devour the world
or, from here to the horizon,
scribble a simple name:

ant ant ant ant ant ant

But more than a scavenger,
the ant is an agriculturalist.
Herself, a minute tractor,
her fields, the gallery

walls within the hill,
she cultivates a fungus,
a dark harvest
she reaps without a song.

Against the ant, tradition
holds this one complaint:
when winter rolled in
and its white artillery

blanketed the countryside,
she barred at her gates
where it froze to death
the jongleur of our meadows,

the improvident grasshopper
for having fiddled away
the whole green season.
Food for thought to us fiddlers

(food for the ant come spring).

Crowned by the dark
halo of despair,
the angel sought solace
in some far flung corner
of the universe.
What he felt was new:

Eve is nowhere in sight
and still he sees her,
in the garden, by the creek,
as she lifts her arms
to reach (oh loveliness)
the nest in the tree.

His angel mind in disarray,
wings, muddied and in tatters,
he plucks his lyre
not in praise of God
but, for the first time,
to strum out of grief
this mournful song.

It sums our vital force and our will.
Cowards had theirs sliced and in Sparta
teachers bit those of lazy students.

It was with his imperial thumb
that the Emperor condemned or spared
the vanquished. "The thumb *is* Man"

wrote d'Arpetigny and was right:
idiots have very short thumbs,
new born babes, as yet lacking will,

hold theirs in the closed hand
as do the epileptic, the paralytic
and, of course, the dying.

Desbarroles claimed to have seen
the sign of eroticism in a hand
where the thumb had a phallic shape.

Over-sized thumbs belong to genius:
in politics: Robespierre, Napoleon;
in painting: Raphael, Correggio, Gandava;

in literature: Milton, Shakespeare, Dumas
(the elder), Musset and George Sand.
If the thumb is large and spatulate

the owner has a marked preponderance
for sombre sadness, a love for soil,
a strange delight in crypts and mines.

If the thumb is badly shaped, twisted,
it is the thumb of shameful celebrity:
famous criminals, whores, perverts.

The round thumb is resolute; or resigned.
It is often found in Brittany.
The elementary thumb, thick, massive,

earthy, is the thumb of the peasant.
This sort of thumb abounds in Lapland.
The vulgar thumb is striking for size

– either too large or too small –
and for the hint of malformation.
It corresponds to simple tastes.

As to the presence or absence of hair
a rule to keep in mind is the useful
Vir pilosus aut libidinus aut fortis.

Balzac: the lines where our flesh ends
and the nail begins, contain the mystery
of our fluids transformed into horn.

If the thumb-nail is defective
it could be a sign of bronchio-pulmonary
suppurations, according to Parmentier.

If the nail is short, covered with flesh,
it often denotes sensuality, ambition.
If it is simply short: irony.

The dark nail marks the fatal mystic,
the roseate nail, the optimistic,
curved nails, the perpetually hungry.

The thumb is ours to decipher and oppose.
The inclinations printed on the thumb
contest the vagaries of the free willed heart.

A PRINCE

The brain comes out via the nose.
Just so. The cranial cavity is cleansed
at the river before it is crammed
with aromatic weeds. Dead he will forever
hear that river, smell the breeze on its shores.
He has become more than the ignorant prince now:
he is a meadow in the full buzz of sunlight.

Thoughts? None ever troubled that clear brow
and now, as he sails towards the light,
it would be unseemly were he to acquire
such a habit in the afterlife.

TRAPEZE

I go to her.
Sometimes
she comes to me.

Below us
the earth moves
as it must.

Hormones, hydraulics,
gravity, what not ...
the quick arc

that takes us
from dressed to naked
in nothing flat.

But surely more.
Lost in celestial
ruminations, Rilke

told lovers to move
beyond the body
as if, in doing so,

they could enter
the locked gates
of a holier realm.

The metaphysics
of flesh and bones
and skin and hair

seemed lost on him
who could not see
that fragile, transient,

perishable
though they be,
our bodies

are in no need
of transcendence:
moving together

they manifest
such power
as allows

two beings
to let go
the trapeze of self

so as to rise
– blessed acrobats –
fully naked

together from one bed.

Sweetie, consider Spinoza:
pleasure, he wrote, accompanied
by the idea of an external cause
is love. So there you have it:

yours, the pleasure, naked in my arms,
while I, delighted, its external cause
who, in bringing you your pleasure,
am given such pleasure in return.

So there we have it: in the alternating
circuitry of this bed, taking pleasure
then being its cause are roles
lovers, all too gladly, exchange.

THE FISH

The fish gleamed
in my hand,
stared hard at me
and said not a word.

I questioned him:
what secrets did he hold,
what green depths ...
He said not a word.

Again I questioned him:
the horoscope of sirens
read in the slow
drift of starfish,

the melancholic key
of the whale's song ...
But he said not a word.
Sarcastic, I asked

if he had enjoyed the bait,
whether the silver hook
had been barbed
to his satisfaction.

Then I turned to threats:
frying pan, boiling oil,
a vision of his bones
scattered to seven cats.

The fish gleamed hard
inside his silver silence
and kept one eye fixed
inexorably on me

though I promised
to return him to the waters
for one word, any word,
harsh as it might be.

ELEPHANT ROCK BEACH

Perhaps it had been the beers,
the droning sun or slack slap
of waves that hauled him, asleep,
to beach him, younger by decades,
on some Brazilian shore.

But brought back by the quark
of these scavenging gulls,
he was startled at being himself
(and more!) with a wife and son.

In the dream it had been he
who played with bucket and shovel
surrounding himself with turrets
while his parents dozed and droned.

This by far the stranger dream:
that he should now awake
in English, conscious of a life
that does not appear his own.

In the shallows, the grey rock
turns in a wash of kelp and foam
and he knows that in a moment
it will spout them awake
and they can all go home.

THE POET READS TO HIS BELOVED

In *The poet reads to his beloved*
the beloved is seized by restlessness.
They sit on the carpet, facing each other
but she is anxious, as if expecting flight.

The caliph holds the vellum
that holds his words of praise:
He praises the fullness of her buttocks,
compares her breasts to pomegranates.

The beloved smiles at the pleased caliph,
the startled almonds of his eyes –
but her thoughts, well her thoughts
lie elsewhere: the beloved is *in absentia;*

though now, as she reaches for the rabbits
and begins to stroke their ears
for no reason she can fathom
tears begin to form and he stops reading.

Defunct though it appeared to be, they felt
the proper setting might make love return
long enough to lend to their finale
a touch of tenderness, of bitter grace,
a chance, who knows, at a rapprochement.
Thus, this little *déjeuner sur l'herbe*
with the oak as their sole witness
where they recall vows that crazy-glued them
one to the other at Golden Gate Park.
Remember, she said, our weekend in Nice?
Nice is nice, he thought of the discarded
line of a poem left unfinished.
Recall, he asked in lieu of answering,
the morning I called you from an airport?
I was in Paris, booked on to Seville
trying to sort out what it was I felt:
ten years of marriage and the heart's needle,
– yours and mine – still wavering. You hung up.
At the bar at the Charles De Gaulle I sat
and drank then changed flights and returned to you.
So you did. But what good were you to me?
A broken man who did not know himself.
Though I said nothing, I wished you had gone
to spare us both how many years of grief.
The bees hummed by a clump of goldenrod.
The wind ruffled the leaves of the oak tree.
The sun cleared a bank of clouds and shone down.
Nice was nice was how she remembered it.

PLEA BARGAINING

Beginning with Lord,
ending with Amen
I wrote, you may recall,
a note last month

in which I asked
with appropriate humility
for a re-negotiation of contract
where, without prejudice,

you would ease certain burdens,
I would desist from certain claims.
I have not had your answer
and am, I must say, perplexed

not just by your silence
but by these added griefs
you've now chosen to inflict:
the laming of my left leg

days before I was to leave
for Greece, a low blow
which I took in stride;
the strife you made rise

between the wife and me
all cannot but exacerbate
already strained relations.
Because I do not see

Saint Christopher
as others might: a saint
who is all brawn, no brain,
but rather as one known

for traversing difficult terrain,
I have named him my intermediary.
He speaks for me on this matter,
having, as they say, *carte blanche.*

Do not, I do beseech you, delay
bringing this matter to a conclusion
satisfactory to us both so that
my next letter can sing your praise.

SOLO FLIGHT

What on earth could you possibly mean
when you call me to call me selfish?
Am I not always ready to spring
into action and come to your rescue?
(Though your SOSs range from the stroke
that winged your father, the pilot,

to hell freezing over when the pilot
on your furnace blew out and a mean
Winter moved inside). What a stroke
of luck (yours!) that though "so selfish"
I left Jean's and raced to your rescue:
a match and presto: soon you had Spring.

Around you I'm a watch with its spring
wound tight or go around numb, on auto-pilot;
I need to implement the most urgent of rescues:
not yours! Mine is what I mean.
You'll call to let me know I'm selfish
then go on and on about his stroke.

If only we could change the tune by some stroke
of magic; we would help each other spring
free of these roles. Pretend we are shellfish:
let's leave our past behind. You won't co-pilot
my life, I'll find within the means
to be more generous, less smug at my rescues.

Who knows whether together we could rescue
him from the black hole of this stroke?
(Though seeing him so helpless makes me feel mean).
You're at a loss with his broken springs
and, washing my hands, I'm Pontius Pilate.
Perhaps you're right. I'm foolish *and* selfish

wishing his ordeal over for entirely selfish
reasons; writing him here as beyond all rescue.
This mission he flies solo, the ram-rod pilot
waiting for the clock's final down-stroke
while glaring we sit, tight as coiled springs.
Perhaps we both should learn to be less mean-

spirited, meaning, I guess, less selfish;
tap proverbial springs of kindness and rescue
from the chamber of his stroke, our loveless pilot.

DUPLEXITY

Not like a broken record;
more like an argument
continually branching, fractal:

the derelict heart
reiterates its forked design.

Where two roads diverge
its choice is not to choose
but to travel both.

Plot that walk
on a graph.
What do you get?

Curves, like hammocks
or, trough to crest,
a series of waves.

In slow motion
a film reveals
the hidden virtues:

subtle undulations,
microscopic curlicues,
eddies of movement

triggered at each
bounce of a step.
So when she moves

away from the pew
the congregation
shuts their eyes

except for the few
who later claim
they saw St. Christopher

drop the Child
so as to follow
unencumbered

her ambulations
out the doors.
Moved myself

I will only say
that when she moves
so fully does she move,

the whole of her is moving
Holy Mother of God!
into unequivocal grace.

By now pronounced, these wings
do not disturb me much
except when a strong wind blows
or strangers ask to touch.

Still, there are advantages:
I'm able on cold nights
to wrap my girl in comfort
while she, in turn, delights

in the erotica of feathers.
Old friends avoid us now
put off by all the fuss.
Engaged by the Moscow

Circus, I stunned those atheists
when under The Arc of Light,
wings extended, I suddenly appeared
between Dwarf and The Lady With a Beard.

LOVE'S VERSO

If at times he feels he could
throttle her or wish her
plunged into the cauldrons
of hell, this too is love

and only those unfamiliar
with love's obverse
might deem such passion
strange. They should note:

while she retains a strangle-hold
on his attention she is,
– though in another house –

so exquisitely conscious of it
the moment is electric –
and his attention repaid in kind.

BABEL

When he struck and splintered
the clear crystal of the earth's

tongue, when he scattered us
in this tide of gutturals,

could he not understand
that here was not arrogance,

but wild-eyed and improvident
love giving shape to its yearning?

BLUE LETTERS

Dear Jody, I write to you
seemingly out of the blue
but not quite: I've read your note
which arrived by mail boat
only yesterday – a full year
since you wrote it but, I swear
I still see you late at night,
lining up the words just right,
losing track of all the hours
spent scouring the thesaurus
for new ways of saying "scum,"
on and on *ad nauseam*.
By the time your words arrived
those feelings had been archived
or you simply let them go
realizing how their slow
corrosive work on the heart
takes its toll. You chose to start
anew. So why should I write
you now, angry or contrite?
Then again, I may be wrong,
knowing you can be headstrong
and nurse this grudge forever.
Either way, would it matter?
Half-heartedly, I wish you well,
knowing you wish me in hell
or, did so a year ago
when all that angry cargo
found freight in your *billet-doux*.

What of me since I left you?
I travelled – then settled here
and may stay another year
or two. I enjoy my place,
the white-washed walls, the terrace
that opens to all the blue
I could ever wish. It's true
that indifference has not come
as it does, it seems, to some.
Still, you're less of an issue:
these days I hardly miss you.

I write this on Saturday
while nearby two donkeys bray
by the soccer field where men
sit and smoke in darkened stands.
Through my open window:
the scent of mint, oregano.
Then, half song and half lament,
– a lover who now repents? –
the arabesque of sorrow
rises from the streets below.
I may send you this or not.
What's the use of getting caught
in a *pas de deux* once more?
No one's asking for an encore.
Friends? No; but perhaps as ghosts
staked out at the outermost
edges of each other's selves
who slip in, sometimes by stealth
or arrive, out of the blue,
(literally!) and typically, off cue.

THE BAPTIST

How my head came to be on that platter?
Mother and daughter had the hots for me.
Something about all those imprecations.
How well I did Old Testament fury:

Language got me rolling and I could curse
with the best: oh you bitch of Babylon!
(This re the mother and me not yet warm).
Salome smiled and whispered John oh John.

How was I to know about the bad blood
between the two? The daughter just assumed
I was coming on to her. I'm not blind
to beauty but knew I was being groomed

to play the fool in the family's feud.
What Sal wants you can bet Sal always gets
and in the euphoria of all those veils
falling around her dancing feet she lets

him know what this little number will cost.
Upon hearing the price, daddy feels lost
but, true to his word, sends off for my head.
I was killed in my nightshirt, lying in bed.

PLEASURE

Unable to choose
whether first to enjoy
with eye or hand
and thus not choosing –

pleasure makes of the eye
a tactile organ
and teaches the hand
that was blind to see.

And with that we begin:
a hum, a hymn,
a string of yeses
that quickly branch into

tributaries of breath
as homage is paid
to and by ourselves.
(Must we have such

pleasure and hear it too?)
Her ladyship's *bateau*
and indeed myself
now fully rigged

ply these rivulets
but sense already,
beyond the delta,
the wide expanse

of a turbulent sea.
Such sharp intake.
Such quick release.
(A chugging of sorts?)

Try this: as if within
some small engine
was turning over
and once it caught

such a thrum followed
that pleasure,
so richly vocalized,
became embodied:

a third presence
– almost distracting –
and yes yes yes it went
as we two came.

TOMATOES

By dint of having to negotiate
the curved roads of this island, the zig-
zags of its mountain paths where switch-
back is followed by switchback
so the view seems continuously the same
yet perspective is constantly altered,

a certain template impresses itself
on the mind: it too begins to rejoice
in the round about. And more: no longer
acknowledges the straight-line traverse
from point A to anywhere but delights
in the meandering any human exchange

such as this one affords. Your purchase
of these five tomatoes, for example,
is contingent on your patience. So relax.
He will have you know that these tomatoes
were grown on land owned by his grandfather
then owned in partnership by five brothers

the oldest of whom was his own father,
a blacksmith, may God take pity on his soul.
One uncle went to Detroit, changed his name,
married, fathered two daughters, then died.
When the body arrived at the airport
and they opened the casket, a blond man,

impeccably coiffed, an American
flag on his lapel, grinned at the family.
They almost sent him back, they were so mad.
Another uncle owns the *Christina,*
that blue and white sailboat, big enough
to ferry forty tourists to a beach hidden

on the lee of the island. He charges
for food, for drinks, for suntan lotion.
He makes a fortune and drinks a fortune
and, twice, ran the *Christina* aground.
The fourth lives in a now empty convent:
caretaker, gardener and tour guide:

visitors ring a bell and he unlocks
the heavy gate, shows them the garden,
ushers them into the coffered chapel
where they pray to a dark, ancient ikon
shaped out of mud and the blood of martyrs
or, foreigners, admire the murky mural

candle soot has over the centuries
practically obscured. The Second Coming:
Jesus, high on his throne, while on earth
graves spit out the startled resurrected.
The youngest uncle had his heart broken.
Lives now in another village. He's tried

to sell his share to the remaining two
but they can't see eye to eye on the price.
The land is stingy, he shrugs, yields little:
some garlic, wild oregano but today
these five tomatoes and, coming round
at last to answer the question you asked

and one you did not, he negotiates
this final switchback to let you know that, yes
the tomatoes are fresh and, hand to heart,
that no, he could not let them go for less.
And five precious tomatoes, one for each
of five brothers, you suddenly realize,

are placed inside the bag and, having listened,
you are now implicated in his life,
in the life of this island that is criss-
crossed as much by paths and winding roads
as by the meandering of stories
eager to find themselves, reader, a new host.

ACKNOWLEDGMENTS

Earlier versions of some of these poems have
appeared in *The Paris Review, Descant, Matrix,
Ploughshares, Pebble, Flyway, Books in Canada,
The Agni Review* and *Queen's Quarterly*.

For suggestions on these poems I am grateful to Aino
Paasonen, Johanne Pulker, Richard Sanger, and Doug
Thompson. I am particularly indebted to Sheila Dwight
for her patience, enthusiasm, and advice through en-
dless revisions of poems and manuscript. The poem
"Dancer" is dedicated to her, "The Baptist" is dedica-
ted to Orde Morton and "Tomatoes" is dedicated to
Michael Harris.